Rapture

Rapture

LOCAL AUTHOR *Claire Krulikowski*

ISBN No. 09708590-5-8
Library of Congress No 2003112596

Cover art "Phoenix Rising"
courtesy of artist Sharon Walker.
For information about the art of Sharon Walker,
email: sharonstarwalker@aol.com

Photographer credits:
Cover photograph of artwork "Phoenix Rising"
taken by West Kennerly.
Author photograph by Beverly Lee.

The First Word Publishing

 247 Pelly Ave N
Renton WA 98055
425-254-8575
Dejonfw@yahoo.com

Dedicated in loving memory
to the sacred life and divine teachings of
spiritual visionary and author,
Jacqueline T. Snyder,
and
to divinity's Z ...
that each of us may know
how loved we truly are.

Rapture

Table of Contents

Introduction

"It is characteristic of the spiritual
that we can only recognize it
when we take the trouble,
at least to a small extent, to become
other than we have been hitherto."

-Rudolph Steiner from "Nature Spirits"

The most intimate relationship we enwrap
our live's within reveals the truest aspects of
whom we most truly believe we are in that mo-
ment. Its ambiance is reflected in the glimmer-
ing light of our grandest expectations for it.

What does this truism say of our individual
relationship with God? What happens to a
woman who falls in love, in rapture, with God?
How does the touch of *that* hand on the flesh of
her life, on the fabric of the world surrounding
her, feel? Where does she and her lover go?
What speaks between them? Who might she
be who savors such a kiss? And what of this
divine Lord who entices a rapture so many oth-
ers have run from?

Pressed between these sheets, the poetry of
such whispered moments reflect and acknowl-
edge a sacred romance and God's greater de-
sire for personal intimacy with each person
willing "to become other than we have been
hitherto." They celebrate a love daring to
speak its name in *this* life whose roots hold the
promise of fulfillment of a holy pledge.

Rapture

I am overcome with a love
which lances my chest
with its soft kiss;
whose lips, felt upon my flesh,
touch my heart,
release gasps for breath;
quickened blood flushes every pore,
washing thoughts and memories from me
of any life but this;
our breath, mingling in sweet converse,
birth dreams entwining heaven and earth
as ecstasy ruptures all our pasts
becoming, *living*, as Christ at last...

Recalled

My head once laid upon his chest
my trust was pure, inviolate.
Lifetimes, centuries, have passed;
he'd left to reign over heavens vast
I'd mourned, then fought to forget.

Rebirthing time and time again
not remembering how or why or when
our paths would one day cross,
in mortal flesh resigned myself to loss
I'd mourned, then fought to forget.

Born both to high and lowly states
my life seemed such an unholy fate;
I sought the beauty of my bride
giving my heart to those few eyed
I'd mourned, then fought to forget.

Shattered spirit, broken-hearted,
how far the journey since we'd parted;
still not grasping rhyme or reason
finding no solace, receiving no vision
I'd mourned, then fought to forget.

This life I'd turned the other way
sacred entreaties kept at bay;
not caring for advice of priests
all belief in prayer ceased
I'd mourned then fought to forget.

Oblivious to holy thoughts
success and status all I sought;
Why choose *now* to talk to me
of promises yet still to be
I'd mourned, then fought to forget.

Yet my heart and soul rejoiced
hearing love for me re-voiced;
this is the moment long awaited
long desired, unsatiated
I'd mourned, then fought to forget.

Newly risen from my sleep,
joy awakens me to weep;
my Lord returns to take me home
God's message lies within this poem
I'd mourned, then fought to forget.

Remember, waken, do the deed
all of us must take the lead;
"These...and greater deeds you'll do;"
parables recalled by few
I'd mourned, then fought to forget.

This voice so strident, eyes so true
frightened, thrilled me, and renewed
what otherwise might aught have died
strangled in the web of lies
I'd mourned, then fought to forget.

Now tender caresses yield
much more love than hate has healed;
the spiral of our life's caress
beckons more than ever guessed
I'd mourned, then fought to forget.

God has promised to us all,
responding to our agreement's call,
heaven shall reign upon this earth
so look beyond the mortal birth
you've mourned, then fought to forget.

Each night I lay me down to sleep
praying to God my soul to keep
entwined within the arms of One
whose eternal love I've won
Recalled, never to forget.

Unclothed

Carry me my Lord, I pray,
let me be at One again
my head resting upon your chest
my heart a gift of your request.

I feel fall from every pore
sweat of my body and yours
delights of passionate caress
sweet tastes of holy perfumed flesh.

Unclothed from this skin of mine
God's son and I are free, entwine
soaring as dove's rise in flight
and feathered fingers tempt more height.

Rocketing towards a golden sea
exquisite pleasures burn through me
as my Lord's passion burst within
unleashing all I've ever been.

How many more grant He such bliss?
How many souls more does He kiss?
He'll nourish all who seek His bed
Divinely fed, none leave unwed.

Lying In The Arms Of God

Desire pulls me from my bed
where I've lain so long unwed.
I raise my arms
surrendering
and feel new blood beat
within me.

As my will succumbs to this
my strength is fed by our first kiss.
I lift my heart
in offering
while flames lick every
part of me.

What is this blessing I've received
which I devour on bended knee?
I raise my eyes
questioning
and liquid light
answers me.

God's Holy Spirit reigns so bright
my life's transformed by its might;
my soul arises
finally freed
to grasp the Promise
offered me.

Long ago the Promise made
long ago our debts were paid
awakened memories
call to me
to love all others -
Be as God.

Belief's Bright Joy

I have traveled far and wide
to view the sources of joy's life
standing always by
a great Light.

The world that I have eyed
colors like a new-wed wife
as belief springs spry
to sights bright.

My belief's deep sigh
no longer sounds doubt's strife
nor unleashes a cry
in dark nights.

The soul can't long hide
impassioned desires of the like
divine beauty's bride
sings of God's holy sight.

God Speaks

It is summer – August -
but warmth this evening has "gone south."
A cold autumnal wind bundles me
beneath blankets on the lounge chair
in my yard.
Grey clouds, thick as down comforters
bundle the heavens out of sight.
Dried Maple leaves,
dead before their time,
release
and dance their last dance around me,
swirling from their favored perch
to ground zero.

I laugh,
watching them spiral,
witnessing my prayers answered on a breeze
seeing
God's meteorological metaphor made manifest.
I delight
because I know,
like leaves discarded from a tree,
much that's old has released from me.

Beholden

Beholden to the sacred grove
I step lightly, bowing low
feel the earth beneath bared feet,
mist-dampened soil smelling sweet
I let my prayer rise on a breeze
humbled always to my knees.

Sensing the promise of new life
the need to end all worldly strife
feeling new love for all I see
I act in ways making this be
and let others reflect this back
filling the gap ending all lack.

Simple, soft, God's voice repeats
in such as these mere human feats;
a change of thought, new truth spoken
feeling new heart, our souls woken
grasping each new revelation
we are reborn, fed on this potion.

Silent messages as sweet
draw me to this grove to eat
sensing unseen kin all round
delighted by this peace I've found
I drink entreaties gifted me
to describe divinity.

Stepping lightly, bowing low
I depart this sacred grove
feel the earth beneath bared feet,
mist-dampened soil smelling sweet
hear other prayers beyond the trees,
our chorus rises on the breeze.

Only One

Only One will raise me up!
I pledged my soul this long ago
each life seeking His cup to sup.

Like a knight before his Lord
now on bent knee bowing my head
I await the blessed sword.

When it falls then I am raised
to gaze upon my true love's face
overcome, I reel, feel dazed.

Dazzling fount of divine grace
these intoxicating eyes, as jewels
enrich, bind me in tender lace.

I'd felt I'd waited far too long
despairing to be left again
yet now my soul erupts in song.

As my beloved Lord takes me
we ascend as our lips kiss
waves thrust us towards heaven's sea.

When at last I draw a breath
my life's consequence is birthed
relinquishing all fear of death.

I've journeyed to return within
this womb of nurturing embrace,
desire wakened beneath soft skin.

"Yet, why for me this destiny?
My head and heart's oft battled it,"
I ask the One who's chosen me.

Silence meets this weak request.
Why, how could I even ask?
When will my doubts be put to rest?

Despite such swirlings in my brain
my Lord's eyes still my countenance
comfort and heal these mortal pains.

"Remember" whispers infinite
worthiness of my soul's life
whose flame my Leige first lit.

Flames of my soul's memories
reveal truths my ego'd hid,
such wisdoms gained, dismay leaves.

Through time's spiraling corridors
I've quested for God's Promises
oft given up, angered and sore.

Yet nothing matters except this!
Seeking to live this life as Christ
returned me to this blessed bliss.

This knight now basks within the Light
holy, sweetened, sustenance
whose dreams have fed me each life's night.

The One long sought has raised me up
acknowledging my pledge fulfilled
outstretched hands offer His cup.

I fold myself within the Soul
whose beauty ravishes cosmos,
accepting Him's been my sole goal...

Who Love I?

No man can see what throbs in me,
the protoplasmic ecstasy
that sings

Songs, currents, poised then spin
delicious, tender skein
so sweet

I yield to feel the more within
light meandering fingers bode no sin
but tease

rekindle senses long untouched
forgotten in my sleep
this life

now, wakened to be realized,
wonder who love I?
My God!

The Romance

My heart can feel the mystery
a lace-like string leading me
ever nearer to Whom I love.

Singing songs on swirling winds
lighting lamps of morning dew
floral fragrance entice me near.

My skin's a leaf caressed and teased
emotion sweet, exposed, drunken
olfactory desires plead.

Lying on our bed of earth
we two as one commune and move
I the vessel worked within.

Breath drawn, I cry that others feel
this thrilling divinity
bare flesh and blood's soulful embrace.

I release the last of me
and await the pleasured choice
yearned for so long before this life.

Co-mingling, our poised spirits cry
explosive light tears flesh from me
transforming mortal blood to wine.

Awakened as if new to life
my blue sky lover's eyes kiss mine
revealing all still held within.

These secrets passed between shared breath
unfold petaled lips to bloom
bright as morning flowers bedewed.

I yearn to bask beneath this glance
but I'm told it's time I go
and teach others this sacred right.

Such pleasure will be mine and yours
prophetic glory to reveal
God's love to all humanity.

Grace...of God

The fever of our parting lips
burns every place she had embraced
still these many, many years since
first her eyes enticed me
with their sparkling dance.

My passionate, unbridled youth
knowing more than time had taught
and less than truly wrought
threw its ravenous blood
boiling upon her fire.

Rising, erupting, torching the sky
the startled sparks of enjoined souls
spoke indiscriminate secrets
for all listening to hear
of destiny's desire.

How is it we'd returned to be
so different and desiring
to birth new life within our wombs,
heaven upon God's earth
immaculate concept.

Mystery, not fantasy
speaks in hollows of this flesh
urging me suckle wisdom
of God's fountainous grace
from these sacred breasts.

My hungered thirst is never quenched
and drinks the sea, sun, and green grass
feeling her now held within
the blanket of my skin,
old memories converse.

Life's now lived another way
her urging presence lights the flame
of warmed fires in the night
making dark now bright
transforming us in God.

Yet still under celestial skies
each sparkling star wakes particles
recalling our first covenant
to live Realized...
the touch of this first kiss.

Knight Of My Soul

Sometimes I dance with
the knight of my soul
like a courtesan,
seeking to stir desire and
tempt this flaming beauty
from its unspoken duty
with the mortal desires
of my life's flesh.

I dream, I tease,
I wake unbedded.

On other eves I kneel
before this regal knight
like a vessel virgin
with downcast eyes fearing
the imagined touch
that will rend forever
the fabric of who I've been
and leave me forever...disfigured.

I dream, I cry,
I wake unblemished.

Then, too, I've faced the knight,
shouted a bold challenge
across the jousting field,
donned armor and battlement,
set a steed full speed
heedless of my fate,
too late realizing my knight
meant merely to step aside.

I dream, I fall,
I wake confused.

I try to reason with the knight,
over tankards my logic's sound
yet no matter how hard
I pound my fist to prove the point
across from me a smile's
the only response I seem to raise.
I wonder if this knight's naïve,
a simpleton, or...is it me?

I dream, I argue,
I wake bemused.

Finally I lie, curse, cheat to prove
how clever I can be and maybe stir
if only a single reprimand
from so aloof a one as this
yet this knight doesn't question
or turn from or against me
and, finally, I realize and accept
my soul's ardent love of me.

I dream, I surrender,
I wake betrothed.

Now within each other we breathe
the beating of our hearts as one;
how silly to have fought
my own soul's loving embrace,
to recall hiding behind so many masks
and playing so many games
when all along my knight's known
exactly who I am.

I dream, I love,
I wake reborn.

The Face

Paintings written on the sky
by wisps of clouds passing by
reveal meanings which our eye
alone can't comprehend

as spirit beyond our flesh can feel
desires the mind cannot reveal
that humbles body, soul to kneel
how can we comprehend

and step beyond illusive forms
ignore our ego's stubborn storms
expanding beyond physical norms
seeking to comprehend

we're more than we believe we've been
not ever really born of sin
our heritage, divine Kin,
helps us comprehend

the mystery of God's saving grace
entwined within our cell's fine lace
all of us will see The Face
after we comprehend

I AM

The river is my destiny
as in the earth, so within me
as one mingling divinity
I AM

Reflective of God's sacred light
both source and current, day and night
of One whose love song I recite
I AM

Ready to fulfill grand prophecies
living good thoughts, and words, and deeds
and standing strong whilst on my knees
I AM

Beyond life's time flow everpresent
within this form I have been lent
rebirthing, learning what God meant
I AM

Recalling, using, wisdoms taught
creating new realms with my thought
upon earth, heaven's what I've sought
I AM

Coming to know all that has been
and will be, the end of sin
all God's creatures of one Kin
I AM

One drop of water in the stream
nourished by the divine beam
each tributary sews the seam
I AM

Life's Creation

In my meditative eye
I'm assured by purple skies
God's presence oversees my thought
yet lets it wander where it ought.

My will creates the life I know
I take the praise and blame I sow;
good thoughts, words, and deeds so fine
bespeak reminders I'm divine.

Yet, waver often in distraction,
it doesn't matter what ill action
my life toward mastery unfolds
God's love of me ne'er cuckold.

As stalwart, true, your love of me
I'll hold myself, God, unto Thee
my life to bring hope, love, and mirth
and doing so, heaven to earth.

Seeded Need

Day and night my mind's alert,
desiring to quench a hungered thirst.

Mysteries sipped from tree boughs,
a child's hug ignites love now.

Bird songs urge me spread my wings,
new life's the bud a spring rain brings.

My smile lightens another's load,
caring thoughts clear their rough road.

The sun feeds light within my cells,
my spirit digests wisdoms it tells.

A flower petal opens my heart,
the air, my skin never part.

To heal poor's lack, give all I can,
And speak words inspiring belief again.

Christ spoke about the mustard seed;
to live his deeds is this seed's need.

Consequence

In the play of shadow and light
people dance
all believing "we're right"
regardless of the consequence.

The dance is one we learn quite young
to judge
all others except us wrong
held captive to our grudge.

We become enraged each day
at things
others do in their own way
our own egos crown us kings.

Yet what does such judgment mean?
Do you think
we're lost in our wakened dream
intoxicated on pain, as drink?

I've worn this self-same angered mask
not knowing
the many harms my hard tasks
wrought and left me owing.

Such thoughts, words, and deeds exemplify
core beliefs
breeding desires making others cry
and turn other's joy to grief.

This lends discordant rhyme to life
people cower
seek to avoid tongue-thrust knives
or turn, revealing their desire to skewer.

Then thrust, parry, fencing back and forth
this dance
drains our life's meaning of all worth
habitually stuck in circumstance.

Links of chains forged in early years
patterns woven of some other's fears
reflect our own doubt's tears
upon the lives of our peers.

Nothing good's ever come of this
look at
the shattered dreams of your life's abyss
who, tell me, *who* gains from that?

"Dropping the knife from my grasp,"
you say,
"unarms me as beliefs collapse;
I must attack or be made to pay!"

Yet what fate is worse than this
self-made
world pain of great disappointments
through which we curse others to wade.

There was One who came so we'd know
through His
life and death we could say "no"
Salvation whispered: "It is finished."

The suffering, fears, karmic play
binding humanity
he shattered on that sacred day
we're free, find other ways to be!

Purposeful each action of His life
as ours
to eliminate from earth all strife
discover and own our divine powers.

Knowing he's paid our heavens gate fee
and is
our savior reveals God's prosperity
all the wealth we earn flowing from Him.

Blessed forever our children's path
knowing peace
each person's love transforming wrath,
our lives as Christs cause hate to cease.

To manifest God's prophecy
we dance
whilst doing good deeds on bended knee
and manifest new consequence.

Each thought we think creates new realms
now cast
your light so bright no shadow overwhelms
your happiness, new visions vast.

Tell Me

Reader. . .
Tell me I'm not crazy
Tell me my love is real
Tell me you feel God move
in spaces within you.

It's hard to tell another
So hard to feel alone
So hard to hide a truth
so wonderful to know.

I offer you my stories
I offer you my heart
I offer God's own message
and some will only laugh.

Someone urged, "Don't rhyme."
Someone scoffed, "God who?"
Someone said, "Too old."
Another laughed, "Who cares?"

It's hard to tell another
So hard to feel alone
So hard to hide a truth
so wonderful to know.

One woman read "Recalled"
One woman sat and wept
One woman helped me know
the value of this work.

Reader...
Tell me I'm not crazy.
Tell me *our* love is real
Tell me how God fills
these spaces within you.

Reverence

Brow to brow
all secrets known,
gives and takes
this moment's now.

Soul to soul
new wisdoms birth,
gives and takes
our karmic toll.

Holy light
born within,
gives and takes
God's divine sight.

Morning Sight

Silence,
      mythic, bold
erupts between songs of morning birds

Fog,
      omnipotent, mysterious
gleams bejeweled by rays of dawn's sun

Life,
      grand and simply sweet
breathes meaning to me in these...

Breath of Life

Rising in the early morn
woken by a gale wind
watching cedar branches dance
Spirit moving o'er the earth.

Currents of change move on such breeze
What message does it stir to life?
What purpose does it bring to me?
Can I accept God's offering?

Be here today, glad as the wind
moving where God's current dares
touching all, none unaware
of a Presence surrounding them.

It's magical to breathe the life
that moves from the lungs of God,
from God's spirit into mine
every breath a drink divine.

Every morn I am reborn
every day there's deeds to do
every day some place to be
where God's breath carries me.

A Moment

Sanctify yourself
your place of work
your place of rest

Let these be for you
all you wish
your complement

Peace and solace reign
in this space
reflect your heart

Candle flames eternal
emit God's Light
drowning the dark

Pure intent of prayer
divine wishes
touch God's heart

A moment's ceremony
birthing change
of consequence...

The Call

Held suspended beyond time
my soul's messenger helps guide
the evolutionary tide
I ride.

This covenant 'tween God and me,
illusive as it sometimes seems,
beguiles and prods a memory
to BE .

What meaning is my life to have?
This question's one I often ask,
and how may I alleviate
world pain?

This desire's fed and watered
in sacred fountains of my calling
to live upon this earth as Christ
again.

In visions I have knelt within
the body of God's heart and soul
felt and seen Love's whole beauty
expressed.

Ne'er again will I forget
the light linking each life to that
holy sphere of God's loving grace...
that Face.

The sight of my eternal soul
standing noble before God
then bending down upon one knee
is sweet.

If visions as sugarplums
spark delight within a child
how much more joy this sight of mine
in me?

Sacred moments attend to all
for we rest gently in God's palm
living renewed trust and faith -
Our Call.

Beyond The Beyond

What lies beyond all that I see
bright sky, star light, majestic sea;
the same exists in me.

Jeweled waves flow and burst
colored tapestries on earth;
the same formed me at birth.

Set your sights on infinity
beyond, beyond...see divinity;
the same calls us to be.

This Bliss

My brother holds me close
A cheek falls upon his chest
happily at rest
no greater bliss than this.

God's lessons told in parables
when spoken to those gathered round
don't teach what I have found
such joyous love as this.

His palm will sometimes brush my hair
and I draw his breath in mine
an intoxicating wine
urging more of this.

How easy to surrender
mortal flesh much less my soul
for the greatest goal
divine reward of this.

Will that others come to know
how much is missed by holding back
Free yourself from lack
And drown yourself in this.

Quest

My God,
What is life supposed to be?
And what of me?
How do I fit in your divine scheme?

My God,
What am I to do and how?
What of my vow?
How may I inspire people *now*?

My God,
Won't you send me holy vision?
Why no mention?
What exactly is my mission?

My God,
Why don't you save the world today?
Is your hand stayed?
"How can I help?" is all I daily pray.

My God,
Will you accept my offerings?
These poems I sing?
Or...have *you* gifted to *me* these rings?

My God,
What good can such musings do?
My point of view?
What greater deeds may I do for you?

My God,
Have I missed the time somehow?
Or...Is it now?
What more fulfills my vow?

When Veils Lift

God, let me know how it will be
when there is no suffering
when doubt, and fear, pain disappear
when veils lift from all we see.

Why do we hold such memories?
Surely these aren't all there is;
creation of such hardship
lacks the grace of divine ease.

Will belief in peace bring true relief?
Can I forgive what went before?
Why can't I try to be like Christ
and live a life of living faith?

If I imagine every day
and allow my soul to speak
my little world becomes transformed
by living life in a new way.

God, let me know how it will be
when people cause no suffering;
when faith, and love, joy lift the veil
and change realities we see.

Why Should I Believe In God?

"Why should I believe in God?,"
came their harsh question,
causing me to draw hushed breath,
wond'ring what was meant.

Yet sensing no irreverence,
just their desire to know,
left me wond'ring what to say,
and trying to recall.

Visions of creation
overpower me.
Should I remind them of the sun
that feeds them everyday?

The miracle of each babe's birth?
The voice that speaks to me?
Would they accept *anything*
I might say to them?

I ask if they will draw a breath
and each of them do.
"What more is there to believe?
God's inside of you."

Gratitude

The night sky was alive with light
as Jacqueline passed from sight
prepared, rising to take her place
and set a smile upon God's face.

The promise made, appointment kept
so proud for her yet I wept
desiring to keep this beauteous being,
praying for her mortal healing.

Knowing God's love drew her near
helped those of us who held her dear
who never believed she'd ever leave;
yet shock turned *faith*, our *hope* to grief.

"This is the way," the Lord whispered,
lovingly Jacqueline released
so we could take our strength from her
and trust in Spirit, not matter.

(Written in gratitude for the gifts given in Jacqueline
Snyder 's passage. She chose her miraculous moment
on the evening of July 4th, 1998 as fireworks lit the cele-
bratory sky. Let us all be the teachers she said we're
meant to be; let us be God's spirit upon God's earth.)

Whispering In Your Womb

Mother, hold me in your arms
like Mary held her babe
and imagine the future
I can create because
I am...
a child of God.

Other books by Claire Krulikowski

Moonlight on the Ganga

An intimate memoir of a sacred journey
along India's "River of Life."
Available at book stores and on line.
(Daybue Publishing; 2001; non-fiction)
www.daybue.com

To order **Rapture**, contact:

Claire Krulikowski
1420 NW Gilman Blvd #2607
Issaquah WA 98027

www.clairekrulikowski.com
claire@clairekrulikowski.com